FOLK CONCERT
CHANGING TIMES

POEMS BY

JANET RUTH HELLER

*Janet Ruth Heller
August 24, 2012*

ANAPHORA LITERARY PRESS

COCHRAN, GEORGIA

ANAPHORA LITERARY PRESS
163 Lucas Rd., Apt. I-2
Cochran, GA 31014
www.anaphoraliterary.com

Book design by Anna Faktorovich, Ph.D.

Cover Image: Joan Baez and Bob Dylan at the March on Washington, 1963, photograph by Rowland Scherman.

Book Proofreading: Katherine Weikel

Published in 2012 by Anaphora Literary Press

Folk Concert: Changing Times
Janet Ruth Heller—1st edition.

ISBN-13: 978-1-937536-26-8
ISBN-10: 1-937536-26-2

Library of Congress Control Number: 2012939912

FOLK CONCERT: CHANGING TIMES

JANET RUTH HELLER

DEDICATION

This book is dedicated to all of the friends, teachers, and family members who encouraged me to write poetry and made helpful suggestions for revisions.

ACKNOWLEDGMENTS

"Traffic Stop in January." *Traffic Stop* (chapbook). Georgetown KY: Finishing Line Press, 2011. 1.

"Getting My Mouth Washed Out." *Michigan Reading Journal* 42.1 (Fall 2009): 62; rpt. in Janet Ruth Heller. *Traffic Stop* (chapbook). Georgetown KY: Finishing Line Press, 2011. 2.

"Skinny-Dipping, July 1960." *Traffic Stop* (chapbook). Georgetown KY: Finishing Line Press, 2011. 3.

"On Using My Mother's College Textbook." *Anima* 7.1 (Fall 1980): 18.

"Sacrament." *WomanSpirit* 3 (Winter 1976): 21; rpt. in *Our Mothers' Daughters*. Ed. Judith Arcana. Berkeley CA: Shameless Hussy Press, 1979. 60; rpt. in *Red Flower*. Ed. Dena Taylor. Freedom CA: The Crossing Press, 1988. 3; rpt. in *Moon Days*. Ed. Cassie Premo Steele. Columbia SC: Summerhouse Press, 1999. 139; rpt. in Janet Ruth Heller. *Traffic Stop* (chapbook). Georgetown KY: Finishing Line Press, 2011. 17.

"For My Father." *A Magazine* 5 (1981): 6.

"Valentines." *Studies in American Jewish Literature* 6 (Fall 1987): 169-70.

"Lovenotes." *Traffic Stop* (chapbook). Georgetown KY: Finishing Line Press, 2011. 4.

"Lovenote I." *Cottonwood Review* 24 (Spring 1981): 3.

"Lovenote II." *Heresies* 3.4 (Spring 1981): 81.

"Attempted Eviction." *The Literary Review* of *The Chicago Maroon* 26 September 1980: 19; rpt. Janet Ruth Heller. *Traffic Stop* (chapbook). Georgetown KY: Finishing Line Press, 2011. 5.

"Second Spring." *Traffic Stop* (chapbook). Georgetown KY: Finishing Line Press, 2011. 6.

"Anti-War Rally, Madison, Wisconsin." *Poets and Peace International* 3 (1983): 39.

"For Mary Vecchio, August, 1973." *Canticum Novum* 1 (1973): 75.

"An Elegy for Phil Ochs." *Journal of Popular Culture* 10 (Spring 1977): 547; rpt. in *San Fernando Poetry Journal* 3.2 (Winter 1981): 56; rpt. in Janet Ruth Heller. *Traffic Stop* (chapbook). Georgetown KY: Finishing Line Press, 2011. 10.

"Anti-MacNamara Demonstration." *The San Fernando Poetry Journal* 3.2 (Winter 1981): 53; rpt. in Janet Ruth Heller. *Traffic Stop* (chapbook). Georgetown KY: Finishing Line Press, 2011. 11.

"Spunk." *Michigan Reading Journal* 42.1 (Fall 2009): 62.

"Officemates." *Traffic Stop* (chapbook). Georgetown KY: Finishing Line Press, 2011. 7-8.

"Spring in Chicago." *The Poet* 15 (1977): n. pag.

"Snubbed." *The Mendocino Review* 8 (1984): 114.

"A Visit with the Dead." *Studies in American Jewish Literature* 22 (2003): 178.

"Wedding Guest." *Wind Literary Journal* 12 (1982): 18; rpt. in Janet Ruth Heller. *Traffic Stop* (chapbook). Georgetown KY: Finishing Line Press, 2011. 12.

"Epigram for the Educational Testing Service." *Kentucky Poetry Review* 21.2 (1985): 40; rpt. in *Women's Glib: A Collection of Women's Humor*. Ed. Rosalind Warren. Freedom CA: The Crossing Press, 1991. 161.

"Learning to Sew at Thirty-Three." *Grand Valley Review* 14 (Spring 1996): 54; rpt. in Janet Ruth Heller. *Traffic Stop* (chapbook). Georgetown KY: Finishing Line Press, 2011. 13.

"Modern Language Association Convention in Chicago." *The Minnesota Review* ns. 48-49 (December, 1998): 15; rpt. in Janet Ruth Heller. *Traffic Stop* (chapbook). Georgetown KY: Finishing Line Press, 2011. 9.

"Autumn Leaves," forthcoming in *Sugar Mule*, July 2012.

"Haunted." *Winds of the World*. Ed. Don Peek. Pittsburg TX: Poetry Press, 1977. 9.

"Clarity." *Women's Encounters with the Mental Health Establishment: Escaping the Yellow Wallpaper*. Ed. Elayne Clift. Binghamton NY: Haworth Press, 2002. 204.

"Meditations on the Prinzhorn Collection." *Judaism* 41.4 (Fall 1992): 424; rpt. in Janet Ruth Heller. *Traffic Stop* (chapbook). Georgetown KY: Finishing Line Press, 2011. 14.

"'The Golden Age of Bronze in China' Comes to Chicago." *Grand Valley Review* 6.1 (Fall 1990): 23.

"Snapshots of the E. R. A. March." *The San Fernando Poetry Journal* 3.2 (Winter 1981): 56; rpt. in *Poets' Voices 1984.* Ed. Kathleen Iddings and others. San Diego: San Diego Poet's Press, 1984. 31.

"Backyard Mystery." *Traffic Stop* (chapbook). Georgetown KY: Finishing Line Press, 2011. 20.

"Indian Summer." *The Pegasus Review* (September/October 1999): 5.

"Olympic Training for Dad." *Traffic Stop* (chapbook). Georgetown KY: Finishing Line Press, 2011. 15.

"Losing My Father." *Traffic Stop* (chapbook). Georgetown KY: Finishing Line Press, 2011. 16.

"Picking Raspberries." *Wisconsin People & Ideas* (Fall 2010): 56; rpt. in *Encore* 38.9 (Summer 2011): 35; rpt. in Janet Ruth Heller. *Traffic Stop* (chapbook). Georgetown KY: Finishing Line Press, 2011. 21.

"Legend" (in "Midwestern Haiku"). *Organic Gardening* January 1985: 138.

"Cherry Trees in Autumn" (in "Midwestern Haiku"). *Recipes for Readers from Michigan Authors and Illustrators.* Grand Rapids: Michigan Reading Association, 2009. 47.

"A Thaw" (in "Midwestern Haiku"). *The Pegasus Review* (November/December 1999): 4.

"Finches in April" (in "Midwestern Haiku"). *Seeding the Snow* (Spring/Summer 2012): 8.

"Clover" (in "Midwestern Haiku"). *Ginyu* No. 47 (25 July 2010): 79.

"Pink Gladioli" (in "Midwestern Haiku"). *Frogpond* 33.3 (Fall 2010): 27.

"Nature's Olympics." *Encore* January 2009: 43; rpt. in Janet Ruth Heller. *Traffic Stop* (chapbook). Georgetown KY: Finishing Line Press, 2011. 18.

"Chihuly's World." *Traffic Stop* (chapbook). Georgetown KY: Finishing Line Press, 2011. 22.

"Showman." *The New Poet's Anthology*. Ed. William Jabonoski. Garden City NY: Cherryable Brothers, 1987. n. pag.; rpt. in Janet Ruth Heller. *Traffic Stop* (chapbook). Georgetown KY: Finishing Line Press, 2011. 23-24.

"The Opera House, Sandwich, Illinois." *Writers at Work*. Ed. Lin Kaatz Chary. Chicago: Chicago Chapter of the National Writers Union, 2005. 23; rpt. in Janet Ruth Heller. *Traffic Stop* (chapbook). Georgetown KY: Finishing Line Press, 2011. 25.

"Snow Poem." *Modern Maturity* December 1981/January 1982: 8; rpt. Janet Ruth Heller. *Traffic Stop* (chapbook). Georgetown KY: Finishing Line Press, 2011. 19.

"Moonstruck." *The Spoon River Quarterly* 7.4 (Fall 1982): 54.

"April Concert." *The Writer* 92.11 (November 1979): 24.

"Folk Concert." *Traffic Stop* (chapbook). Georgetown KY: Finishing Line Press, 2011. 26-27.

CONTENTS

TRAFFIC STOP IN JANUARY
(For Irving Barat)

Rushing to get to work,
I turn left on a yellow arrow,
then see a police car behind me,
flashing lights.
I pull over.

It's ten above,
the crime rate has frozen,
and the Kalamazoo police
need something to do.
I resist the temptation
to suggest that the officer
could shovel the snow
clogging downtown sidewalks.

When I leave the car
to get my driver's license from the trunk,
the officer stiffens,
worried that I have a gun.
He orders me back
into my vehicle.
I comply, annoyed that
a fifty-three-year-old English teacher,
armed with no more than a sharp tongue,
has to get treated
like a hardened criminal.

As he dawdles, I get angrier
and talk back,
telling him he's sexist.
He makes me later and later for work.

I reach the forty-two students
in my women and work class
fifteen minutes late.
But they have all waited.
I briefly explain the delay.
"Tell us the whole story!" they demand.
As I comply, they laugh and I join in,
sharing our vulnerability
to petty harassment.

GETTING MY MOUTH WASHED OUT

Once my grandmother got very angry
when I argued with her.
I was a five year old
who did not know her place.

So she told me to open my mouth
and then she put a bar of soap inside.
Forty-six years later,
I still remember
that awful taste.

But I didn't stop arguing
with her or anyone else.
I've argued with teachers, parents,
rabbis, politicians, and bosses
if they try to limit my freedom
or curtail other people's rights.

I've lived long enough
to see some reforms.
So here's my advice
to other rebellious kids:
if someone threatens you
with a bar of soap,
keep talking so fast
that no one can ever wedge
a stopper in your mouth.

SKINNY-DIPPING, JULY, 1960

Ten sixth-grade girls camp overnight
on the shores of Lake Pokegama
with two counsellors.
After an open-fire cookout and cleanup,
we decide to take a twilight swim
in the dark waters.
Miles from civilization,
we strip naked
and, whispering,
enter the still lake.

I've never swum without clothes before
and welcome the sensation
of cool water on my arms and legs and breasts
and flowing like lava
between my thighs.

CANOE TRIP IN NORTHERN WISCONSIN, 1962

We carry our canoes and backpacks
down the thin strip of land separating the Chippewa River
and Lake Namekagon.
The portage completed,
we eight teenaged girls and one counsellor
re-embark as raindrops begin to fall.

Manitowish campers consider ourselves braver
than Girl Scouts, and we're proud of our canoeing,
having practiced sweeps, pull-to's, rudders, and J-strokes
on an obstacle course back on Boulder Lake.
We've also studied campcraft scientifically,
learning the proper knots for securing tents
and the best ways to build a fire.

So no storm can faze us.
The wind whips across the lake,
shoving waves toward our boats.
We move at a right angle to the troughs.
I'm in the bow, paddling hard
as Tina yells, "Stroke!"
The rain pelts our heads and shoulders,
but we grin and pull up our ponchos' hoods,
looking like monks in the wilderness.

Sandy, our counsellor, leads us in a chorus
of "The Life of a Voyageur."
Judy and I sing harmony.
Lightning saws a jagged edge
across the steel-gray sky.

Timid people would stick close to shore,
but we tough women cut straight across the lake
to find the outlet on Sandy's map.
When thunder booms like cosmic cannons,
we stop singing. We need the breath
for stretching our arms and torsos,
for plowing paddles through the deep water.

Drenched, we reach the outlet
and the more sheltered Flambeau River.
We chat happily, searching for our campsite.

Once there, Ellen and Sue pitch our tents,
I start a roaring fire,
and Gail mixes pizza from scratch
while the shadows gather.

To nine starving women,
the pizza and canned beans
are a gourmet feast.
We swap ghost stories in the dark woods,
then retire to wet tents and damp sleeping bags.
Loons and foxes call in the distance.

ON USING MY MOTHER'S COLLEGE TEXTBOOK

I study from a textbook my mother used.
Its binding has cracked
from two mistresses' demands.

I try to decipher the dreams hidden in her notes
as I add my own.

Three years before my birth,
she underlined
"Those that have children
should have greatest care of future times." *

*From Sir Francis Bacon's essay "Of Marriage and Single Life"

SACRAMENT

Gazing at your newly rounded bosom
and curving hips,
your mother smiles with pride.

When you bare the red fountain
flowing secretly, painfully
from the aroused womb,

she embraces you and whispers,
"This is our shared body
and this our blood."

FOR MY FATHER

You taught me to find Orion
and the North Star, in case I got lost.
At noon we imitated brash jays and crows
and sometimes the mourning dove.

We walked to the nearest park
to feed the ducks and swans.
When I got tired,
we rested on oak logs
you said were hewn by hunters.

Now, pent up in Chicago,
I recall the forests
and your stories about the hunters.
But city lights hide the North Star.

VALENTINES
(For Michael)

In second grade, I carefully pasted
valentines for my hostile classmates.
I handed cards to everyone,
though I felt more hatred
than love for them.

When I was away at college,
my parents mailed me valentines,
neatly timed to arrive on February 14th.
The cards reminded me that I had no lover.

Today you kiss me and pull
a many-colored valentine from your knapsack.
Then you show me how it glows in the dark.

BECOMING A WOMAN

When I was ten,
I found a female nude
in my mother's art book.
The woman reclined on a bed,
her breasts the size of cantaloupes
and her hips like watermelons.

I inspected my narrow body.
Pointing to the picture,
I told my mother,
"Women don't look like that."
"Oh yes, they do," she said.

Slowly, my body changed,
stretching into a miniature version
of the voluptuous creature.
My breasts, the size of apricots,
ached when I lay on them,
and my hip bones thickened
into female curves.

When I was thirty,
I met Michael.
We danced together,
our bodies sometimes touching.
Then he held my hand so tightly
I thought it would break.

He drove me to my apartment.
We kissed in the dark,
and he drew reverent hands
down my torso
from my breasts to my hips.

LOVENOTES

I

I would like to play this evening with you
over and over again
like one of your favorite records.

II

You drew your foot up and down my leg
underneath the bridge table
and I forgot my opening bid,
wondering what you could do
with the rest of your body.

III

On this frozen night,
I wish to gather you
into my arms,
to harvest love
in winter.

IV

I was carried in your arms
into the vortex of a tornado;
the tender torrents of your passion
whirled across me like untamed winds.
My body still spins in your wake.

ATTEMPTED EVICTION

Whereas you have occupied my heart
beyond the terms of your lease;
and whereas you have violated clause four,
which specifies that tenant
must obtain landlord's written consent
before a lock may be installed
on said apartment door;

inasmuch as rent has not been tendered
for landlord's affection
since May of last year,

I hereby evict you from my dreams.

SECOND SPRING
(For Judy and Alice)

Ah! why has happiness—no second Spring?
    —Charlotte Smith, "Written at the Close of Spring," 1784

What is it like in middle age
after the hurt of divorce,
after years of telling everyone
that the institution of marriage
reeks of patriarchy
and just doesn't work,

to look into a male friend's eyes
and see love and longing there
that resemble the passion
in your own heart
emerging from hibernation
and stretching in the sun,

to fall into one another's arms
with this new knowledge,
to have a second spring,
to start over again?

ANTI-WAR RALLY, MADISON, WISCONSIN

Our leaflets have drawn a large crowd. I run into many classmates and a professor I've been trying to reach for weeks.

After the *de rigueur* march to Capitol Square, we submit to the required speeches from familiar organization leaders. But I am sentimental: the cheers of the patient thousands never fail to bring tears to my eyes.

Green Army surplus parkas guard us from the February cold. This irony does not escape us.

Restless, I wander about, joining friends intermittently.

Across the snow-covered grass, two randy dogs make love, not war.

FOR MARY VECCHIO, AUGUST, 1973

María our Comforter,
kneeling, screaming anguished prayer
by the side of the dying Kent student—
at fourteen you descended to Hell
and arose, having conquered Satan
for one indelible moment.

It does not matter
if you play Magdalene in Miami
and caress their distorted bodies
with your blessèd limbs
or enwrap their feet in your angel's hair.

AN ELEGY FOR PHIL OCHS

Your protest songs helped us march through the sixties,
trudging the streets for peace,
an army of noncombatants.

In '76, the bicentennial year,
verses defied your command
to muster into stanzas.
A general deserted by his troops,
you hung yourself in despair.

ANTI-MACNAMARA DEMONSTRATION, UNIVERSITY OF CHICAGO, MAY, 1979

Protestors again crowd the tree-lined Quadrangle as speakers denounce the military-industrial complex. I'm wearing another black armband.

We force our slogan into rhythm: "No award to MacNamara!"

We resurrect the old battle cries: "Power to the people!" "No more imperialist wars!" "Hell no! We won't go!"

Old placards, old arguments, old songs, old boyfriends march through my memory.

Chicago. Madison. Washington. Saigon.

Ten-year-old images melt into today. What has changed? I have come of age.

SPUNK
(For Wendy Nodiff)

As I sat shyly in a back row,
you strode to the front
to give Miss Carpenter
your registration form for seventh grade.

I stared at your petite body,
your sandy hair, your white flats
worn after Labor Day.
I admired your spunk.

You jawboned your way
into the all-male shop class
while the rest of us girls
learned how to sew.

You confronted Leo, the brainy class show off,
without batting an eye.
You started a girls' rowing crew
and served as team captain.

After sophomore year, your family moved away.
I never saw you again.
I miss you, wish we could get together,
and hope you've never lost your spunk.

THE STOPPED CLOCK

The clock has stopped
in my fiction writing classroom
as if it senses
that this group is special.
The students always come early
and ask me questions
as soon as I enter.
When I assign a freewrite,
I can feel the air electric
with young people's energy.
When we discuss Elena's story,
Megan and Eric suggest changes
and we debate them,
making minutes fly.
Together, we drip
collective creative sweat
and swallow time whole.

OBSESSION

I walk down the hall at work
and my boss stares at my breasts.

I go to his office to ask a question
and my boss stares at my breasts.

I speak up at a committee meeting
and my boss stares at my breasts.

I teach a composition class in front of him
and my boss stares at my breasts.

I submit my letter of resignation
and my boss stares at my breasts.

OFFICEMATES

Ed was my first officemate
at Northern Illinois University.
I left student messages on his desk.
But when my students called,
Ed would never take a message.
He smoked and kept interrupting me
to ask how to spell words
as if I were his secretary.
He taught linguistics
and had five dictionaries
on his shelf. After a while,
I pretended that I couldn't spell.

But I complained about the cigarettes.
The next year, the English Department
moved me across the hall
to share an office
with Marcia and Marydale.
They had also complained about smokers.
We bonded like the Three Musketeers
and we formed a support group
to speed our dissertations.
Whenever one of us finished,
the other two treated her
to lunch and hugs
at our favorite restaurant.

Rob became my officemate
at Grand Valley State.
He helped me use the computer.
Comparing notes with tactful Rob
enabled me to keep my temper.
He was always considerate
and moved to a classroom
if our student conferences overlapped.
When the dean threatened the jobs
of untenured faculty,
our office became the War Room
for strategic planning.
We won English Department support
and later convinced the president
to endorse our reappointment.

At Albion College,
I shared a new office with Steve.
Quiet and soft-spoken,
he reminded me of Rob.
We split the task
of clearing the office of debris
left by former inhabitants.
We found homes for five typewriters
and recycled a decade of final exams.
We trusted one another enough
that we chose not to encode
our e-mail passwords.

One semester sharing space with Gail
at Western Michigan University
was more than enough.
Though she studies dance,
she could not enter our office
without crashing into me.
Like a lioness,
she viewed the room as her territory.
Five women used the cubicle,
yet her phone message named Gail
as the sole inhabitant.
Gail talked to herself
as loudly as a football coach
when a referee made a hostile call.

Now I share a ninth-floor office
with Lydia and Anne
and six other colleagues
who drift in and out of Sprau Tower
like Cox and Box in the British play.
After hearing Lydia explain a concept
seven times to a stubborn student,
I conclude that she has the patience of a saint.
The oldest in our complex,
I give advice to the young instructors
on how to avoid overloading a syllabus,
how to get thorough revisions from freshmen,
and how to publish poetry.
At home with these normal people,
I breathe a sigh of relief.

SPRING IN CHICAGO

Skyscrapers mute
the golden trumpet of sunlight.

Greetings are muffled
for fear of retaliation.

The March quickening
in this oasis of culture
yields a harvest
of partial fruit.

SNUBBED

You turned your back to me
at the cocktail party.

I followed suit.

Too proud to speak,
unsure of who should begin,
we stood like two bookends.

A VISIT WITH THE DEAD
(For Mike)

Lost in thought, you drove me to the cemetery.
Cars sped past us on the adjoining freeway
as you searched for the flat grey stone
that marked your father's grave.

You stopped and took my hand.
We stood in silence.

Reading the inscription,
I realized with a shock
that your father's heart
had stopped beating
on my twenty-sixth birthday.
I tried to commune
with a man I had never met.

Although we didn't get engaged
until months later,
that day I think we both
asked for his blessing.

WEDDING GUEST

They wheel the white-haired woman
down the aisle.
A nurse lifts her onto the pew.

Four girls in pink advance, carrying flowers;
then four boys join them.
A girl in white appears.
The woman mutters wildly.

Where is her grand-daughter marching?
What is this familiar chant?
And who is that stranger
in black and white
fumbling with a ring?

EPIGRAM FOR THE EDUCATIONAL TESTING SERVICE

So much depends
upon

a small blue
rectangle

filled in with
pencil

scanned by giant
computers.

LEARNING TO SEW AT THIRTY-THREE

The Sears sewing instructor looks aghast
as my bobbin falls out of its case and rolls into the hall.

A few minutes later, I jam my needle.
Condescendingly, Mrs. Dawson lifts the stubborn implement,
changes the tension setting,
and gives the class a lecture
entitled "100 Ways to Jam an Innocent Machine."

While she shows the advanced students
how to execute a blind hem and embroider floral patterns,
I struggle with simple zigzags
and practice changing the presser foot.

I'm glad she does not know
that I'm a college professor.

MODERN LANGUAGE ASSOCIATION
CONVENTION IN CHICAGO

We fill the Conrad Hilton with culture.
In one ballroom, scholars analyze Jane Austen
while across the hall, Norman Mailer
does a striptease as he reads from his latest novel.

A panel of experts on the twentieth floor
debates whether to teach radical-changing verbs
to conservative freshmen taking Spanish 101.

On the roof, an earnest critic
examines the importance of wind chill factor
in ancient Icelandic sagas.

Linguists compare the communication skills
of higher and lower mammals
while colorless green professors sleep furiously.

Many flock to the Waldorf Room
for an open-bar reunion of German majors
who graduated from Harvard in 1924.

In the corridors, the unemployed
pace back and forth or slump
against the walls.
They revive for the interview,
unpacking their credentials like peddlers.

University presses offer once-a-year bargains
on textbooks and fiction,
selling ideas wholesale.

HAVEN

Weighed down by cares,
I walk along the lake path,
reach a garden
ablaze with red bee balm,
golden torch lilies,
and ten hummingbirds
playing tag–
a slice of Eden.

AUTUMN LEAVES

Leaves like gold coins
fall from the ornamental pear tree
while the tulip poplar sheds
multi-hued flowers.
The sweetgum drops
red and yellow stars.

But oak trees hoard
their dry brown leaves
that rattle in the wind
like my obsessions.

DESERT CHASE

Breathless, I run toward you.
But the desert between us
stretches to the horizon.
Saguaros bend their arms
in gestures of despair.

You call from the distance.
I race toward your figure,
but it is a mirage.
The prickly pear scratches my legs.

We meet at an oasis,
drink from the brook.
You sneer at my torn clothes
and my dust-covered body.
The mockingbird screams.

Under a sky burning
like the scorpion's sting,
we part again.

A PATIENT'S ADVICE

Stop playing God,
you puny doctor!
Stop pretending
that you are never vulnerable,
that you never take risks.

You pose for a portrait of Zeus,
forgetting that like Odin
you have but one eye.

HAUNTED

Doctors flit like bats down the hospital corridors,
congregating at each intersection.
They emit high frequency greetings.
We patients try hard not to stare.

Safe at home, we are pursued
by these mysterious creatures
possessing the tree outside our window,
hanging upside down,
gesturing towards us with shadows.

A TRIBUTE TO SANCHO

You ride through Spain beside me,
my skinny, skeptical Sancho.

Uncomplaining, head uncovered,
you face the wind and rain
I conjure up from memory.

We dine together on hot air
like two penitent Benedictine monks.

You smile at my impossible dreams
as you struggle with your own.

The giants Hope and Fear alternately
gnaw at our innards.

My journey is made tolerable
by your illustrious company.

CLARITY
(For M. C.)

After I talk with you,
the heat wave lifts
and the air clears.

I can see every leaf
on the oaks and maples,
and, drifting from the cottonwood,
a million tiny parachutes.

MEDITATIONS ON THE PRINZHORN COLLECTION OF THE ART OF THE MENTALLY ILL, ON DISPLAY AT THE SMART GALLERY, CHICAGO, APRIL 1985

Graduate students calmly take notes
on the exuberant drawings,
sculptures, paintings, and textiles
of the irremediably insane.

Pohl draws his own head
at awkward angles,
eyes bulging with the fear and anger
that the rest of us try to hide.

Neter's landscape transforms itself
into a witch's head,
the mother/wife/daughter
whom he could never control.

Karl Brendel sculpts wooden men
reduced to head, legs, and phallus
by their mechanized lives.

"Little is known about the women patients,"
the exhibiters helpfully inform us.
Even Prinzhorn's 400-page monograph
merely classifies the women's artwork.
They lack the credentials
of the male artisans.

Men portray themselves standing
on a woman's crotch.
But Elisabeth F.'s pencil captures
a circle of chatting women,
some collapsing.

While a male patient fancies himself the Kaiser,
Else Blankenhorn paints imaginary money
to finance the resurrection of the dead.

Johanna Nathalie Wintsch embroiders a colorful sampler,
imposing decorative order
on a Nazi world gone mad.

A VISIT TO GERMANY

For the first time, I visit Germany,
the home of my paternal great-grandparents.
I love the rolling hills,
the old homes and castles,
the sculptures and paintings,
the street musicians.

I recognize the black locusts in bloom
and all the flowers in my oma's garden:
irises, peonies, roses, pansies, snapdragons.
My family hated dirt tracked into the home,
and here metal stirrups on porches
urge guests to wipe mud off their boots.
My father rarely hugged us,
and here people are friendly but reserved.

Hidden amid the towns we visit
are hints about why my ancestors left
this beautiful and prosperous land.
Every village has a Judenstrasse,
a street for Jews outside the medieval wall
where they would not be protected
from wars or assaults.

Museums have Jewish artifacts:
spice boxes, menorahs,
Seder plates, Torah ornaments.
Yet no postcards feature these objects.
The brochure for Rothenburg
says that Jews left in 1520.
But the pamphlet does not tell why.

My relatives left in 1884,
tired of wars and prejudice.
Brave immigrants to Wisconsin,
working in lumber yards and foundries,
selling insurance, hats, and records,
typing, bookkeeping, waiting on tables,
selling flowers, clerking in department stores,
running a movie theater, building elevators,
selling real estate, printing candy wrappers—
they saved us
from more wars and from the Holocaust.

Kalamazoo lacks the rolling hills
and palaces of Germany,
but its forested plains
offer me a life without fear.

FIRST LOVE
(For Sarah)

You met him at the local playground.
Tall, dark, handsome, and three years older,
Carl joined you on the swings, the slide,
and the roundabout,
which you pretended was the train
from downtown London.
You both called out the stops
between Waterloo and Surbiton.
Then you climbed the rocket together,
laughing and chatting.

Suddenly, he proposed marriage,
took your hand,
led you to a pretend bedroom
under the jungle gym.

We adults grinned.
Your dad asked if the young swain
could wait until you turned four.
Carl's dad told Romeo
that he'd have to sell his toys
to support a wife,
and the future father-in-law
asked the children to write.
Unfazed, you held hands
and played house.

Then it was time to leave.
You bid a wistful goodbye
to your new friend.
Though you searched the playground
for the next few months,
you never saw Carl again.

WEDDING IN EISENACH, GERMANY

We travel to East Germany,
enjoying the rolling hills,
the red tile roofs, the palaces
formerly hidden from Western eyes
by the Iron Curtain.

We stumble upon a local wedding.
After the ceremony,
the bride and groom,
in floor-length gown and tuxedo,
begin to saw a log.
The bride steadies the horse
with her slippered foot.
Each spouse taking one handle,
they work in harmony,
slowly advancing the saw
through the stubborn wood.

At one point, the saw binds.
Calmly, the couple withdraws the saw
and wedding guests help
to rotate the log.
The bride and groom resume
their first joint labor.

When they split the trunk,
the fifty guests cheer and clap.
We join in the applause
for the handsome young spouses
who now face life's problems
as a team.

CAMPING NEAR CUMBERLAND FALLS, KENTUCKY

I. Hiking

Mike chooses the hardest trail in the park.
I pant along behind him
up and down rocky slopes.

I hear rustling among the bushes.
My scream dies away when I see a tiny lizard
fleeing from us two giants. Mike laughs.
"There are poisonous snakes,"
I remind him. He chuckles,
"The rattlesnakes and cottonmouths
are park employees!"

Then we hear water swirling loudly,
reach Eagle Falls.

II. Meals

As we grill steaks,
a red pileated woodpecker
drills for insects
in a tall Southern pine.
Hummingbirds hover over the shadbush,
bees wallow in mountain laurel,
and a young grey squirrel
attacks our garbage bag.

III. Wilderness Library

The rain drones on all afternoon,
confining us to the waterproof tent.
Perched on my sleeping bag,
I read Wilde's essays,
while bourgeois Mike studies *The Wall Street Journal*.
We could do a commercial for the A. L. A.

IV. Insomnia

Still awake at midnight,
I listen for wolves and bears.
Something is clawing the tent,
turning this way and that,
ravenous for food.
Terrified, I burrow in my sleeping bag,
making similar noises, and realize
the "bear" is restless Mike.

CANADIAN ENCOUNTER

Lost tourists, we stop near Kagawong.
An Indian in a broad-brimmed hat drives up
and begins to fish in the lake.
Mike asks him the way to Bridal Veil Falls.
The Indian points to a path through the woods:
"Follow the river," he says.

Like a water snake, the river twists among the rocks,
its rapids too treacherous for a canoe.
We trip on the stony trail,
pass white musk mallow
and orange jewelweed shaped like moccasins.

The falls are worth all our stumbling:
water drops like beadwork from the limestone cliff.
While Mike climbs to photograph the "chute,"
I search for more wildflowers
and find delicate purple bellflowers
enclosed by three Molson bottles.

When we return to the lake,
the Indian is catching a bass.
Mike starts the car.
I wave to the fisherman,
and he waves back.

"THE GOLDEN AGE OF BRONZE IN CHINA"
COMES TO CHICAGO
(The Field Museum, October, 1980)

Pop-eyed dragons curl around a Shang wine vessel
below upside-down cicadas.
Meanwhile, two thirsty tigers
couch at the rim of a Zhou cauldron.
The inscription reads,
"For my second daughter's marriage.
May she live 10,000 years!"

A warrior's curved hatchet
is mounted near a noblewoman's gold-inlaid lamp.
Calmly, terra-cotta soldiers guard the display.

Across the centuries,
American bison stare.

SNAPSHOTS OF THE E. R. A. MARCH, CHICAGO, MAY 10, 1980

The rain stops at 9:30. People sprout like crocuses.
I think Mother Nature supports the march.

Seven-month-old Nathan
teethes on his "Kids for E. R. A." button.

Women professors have come by bus
with peanut butter sandwiches.

The large Nebraska delegation
marches in suffragette formation.

When Betty Friedan addresses the rally,
a hundred thousand people rise.

BACKYARD MYSTERY

Some animal raids our yard at night,
ripping divots in the lawn
like a lousy golfer.

We suspect the fat local groundhog,
but he waddles by day
and doesn't eat grass, worms, or grubs.

Then we suspect the raccoon,
but she eludes us,
except for one visit to our deck.

I stay up late after a snowfall,
peer out the back window.
The full moon spotlights
the culprit: a dark and handsome skunk.

INDIAN SUMMER

When it is seventy degrees in October,
I see everything with the eyes of a child.

The bushes wave arms red as candy
against the sky, blue as a popsicle.
Elm leaves fly past like golden birds
escaping from a fairytale.

The pods of the catalpa
sway in the breeze,
silent chimes
enchanted by a local witch.

Just fallen ginkgo leaves
pile up like doubloons
hoarded by an old pirate.

Fat squirrels hop after chestnuts
before they curl up in burrows
to dream of spring.

At night the moon plays
peek-a-boo
behind the tall buildings.

OLYMPIC TRAINING FOR DAD

Dad, as you grew older
and cancer made you frail,
you hired a physical therapist
and exercised every day,
stretching and lifting weights.

I teased that you were training
for the Olympics
and asked which event
you'd compete in.

During your last year,
you needed a walker
to move around the house.

But two weeks before your death,
you told me that you'd compete
in the long jump.

Dad, now you've jumped
so far away.

LOSING MY FATHER

I lost my father in August.
But how can one misplace
a six-foot-one inventor,
a successful businessman?
When I was a child,
I had to take four steps
for one of his when we walked together.

A few days after Dad died,
I saw three deer behind our home.
The adult deer was very tall
and steered the fawns toward cover.
I wondered whether Dad's spirit
had entered the tall parent.

We used to call him "Daddy-Long-Legs."
Now I can't kill these insects
when they invade my home.

Driving down Crosstown Parkway,
I saw a blue heron in the pond.
Skinny and towering over the ducks and geese,
he resembled my father.

Where are you now, Dad?
I lift up my eyes and see
the stars and constellations
you showed me when I was young.
Are you resting in the Big Dipper?

I miss you.
Hover beside me as I walk,
and when I lose my way,
help me find the North Star.

MARK'S PROGRESS

When Mark was two,
I took him in the stroller
to entertain my nephew
while his parents swam.
He could not say one word,
and he would not look at me
or at the other hotel guests.

But this summer, age six,
Mark can say my name
and talk in sentences
and look me in the eye.
We play dominoes
while we wait for a meal.

Mark holds my hand in the car
and I remember
the Beatles' hit of my youth,
"I Wanna Hold Your Hand."

Skipping, Mark leads the family
as we walk around Elkhart Lake.
I show him ducks and tree swallows,
then teach him to say "seagull."

When we finish the walk,
Mark hugs me
and my cares vanish for a moment
as we both rejoice
in this lifting of the autistic fog
and these newfound social skills.

PICKING RASPBERRIES: LEARNING PERSPECTIVE

I

The black raspberries are ripe
and the golden berries have just turned
from green to orange.

I begin on the east side
of the canes and slowly
work my way west,
picking first the dark purple berries
at eye level and then the ones hiding,
lower and lower, nearly touching the ground.

II

Berry picking is a lesson in perspective:
I would miss most of the fruit
if I refused to lower my eyes,
then stoop and bend.

I push aside leaves and canes
to find the round and juicy globes,
gently pulling the berries
until they fall into my palm.

III

I met three-year-old Braylon at a wedding.
While we waited to eat,
we played peek-a-boo and laughed.
We rang tiny bells
to urge the bride and groom to kiss.
Later, we danced to the DJ's music,
sashaying, jumping, and whirling.

Had I not bent down
to hold Braylon's small hands,
I would not have seen the party
from his point of view.

MIDWESTERN HAIKU

1

Pink gladioli
unfurl in sunshine.
I long for you.

2

Perched in the cherry tree
after a rainstorm,
I float in a sea of gold.

3

The willow's brown hair
has turned grey in the hoarfrost.
The wind combs it back.

4

Corn stubs in winter
bend like Sanskrit
in furrowed scrawls
across the prairie.

5

Rabbit tracks flitter
across powder-light snowfall
like butterfly wings.

6

Twelve inches of snow
overwhelm the crocuses,
seal purple mouths shut.

7

Hoarfrost crumbles, falls
from branches with a clatter
like broken chains.

8

From the sassafras,
finches cross-examine me,
lawyers in red hoods.

9

Clover defies drought
to spread across our backyard.
My love for you grows.

10

Dandelions flutter,
fly away as we approach.
No—golden warblers!

11

Fireflies sparkle
against the green fields.
We startle them
with our Fourth of July display.

12

Cherry tree branches
dance in the wind and dangle
black bead necklaces.

NATURE'S OLYMPICS

Swimmers churn Atlanta pools,
runners streak down dusty tracks,
and gymnasts tumble and fly through the air.
While the Olympic torch burns overhead,
thousands cheer their countrymen.

Here in Michigan, loons paddle near Isle Royale
and laugh like banshees
before they dive and disappear
in the evening mist.
Chipmunks dash across our yard
to capture seeds, stuffing their cheeks,
then scamper toward their burrows.
Goldfinches balance on sunflowers,
chickadees dart from food to swaying trees,
and hummingbirds fly backwards,
landing on titonia like acrobats.

CHIHULY'S WORLD
(For Dale Chihuly)

Your world is curvilinear.
Parts of your sculptures
curl around other shapes
like the tendrils of plants.

In your art, everything becomes
a tree or a flower.
Multi-hued vases on tall pedestals
imitate a silent forest.
You even transform hats
into vibrant yellow blossoms.

Like nature, you abhor a vacuum.
You could simply make a lovely glass bowl.
Instead, you fill the large vessel's inner space
with smaller bowls,
each a distinct form.

You leave bubbles in the glass
and add flakes of different colors,
as if we are viewing the pieces
from the bottom of the sea.

You mount the sculptures on Plexiglas,
which reflects the components,
doubling them like a huge mirror
and incorporating the faces
of us viewers in the gallery.

ANTAEUS
(For Rafael Nadal)

Drawing your strength from the earth,
you arise to combat your foes
on tennis courts around the world.
You serve the ball,
then chase lobs, slices, and overheads
everywhere, never giving up.
You return shots that most players
would consider impossible.
If opponents have tantrums,
you hold your ground,
wait until their demons depart,
then roundly defeat the overgrown toddlers.
When you win, you roll on the clay,
returning to your element.

SHOWMAN
(For Garrison Keillor)

You emerge from the wings
like a skinny frog
and stand on one foot
as the other gym shoe
taps the beat for "Hello, Love."

While Peter O'Struchko's band plays a set,
you vanish from 3,000 peering eyes,
then bound back on stage
to announce your impending remarriage.
Shy Person? Exhibitionist?

Imitating a stalled car in winter,
you and your cohorts provoke laughter
across the frozen Midwest.

You parody the melancholy poems
recited for grade-school pageants
and weave the time warp of Christmas memories,
bound together by the same meals,
the same newspaper photos,
the same family stories.
Your hands wave lyrically to convey the peacefulness
and you lead the audience in "Silent Night."

The stage manager scurries around,
re-adjusting microphones,
carrying last-minute memos
to Chet Atkins and the Ukrainian men's choir.

Gravel-voiced Studs Terkel joins you for a commercial
extolling the magic powers of "Raw Bits."

The live show gallops on:
you look at your watch more frequently
and make broader gestures to cue the musicians.

Six fifty-nine approaches,
and Ukrainians join Southern Baptists
in the last jazzy chorus.

The showman disappears
into his private life.

THE OPERA HOUSE, SANDWICH, ILLINOIS

The old redbrick opera house
had fallen on hard times.
The raked stage no longer shook
with tempests of soprano passion
or the duels of tenor and bass.

The local sheriff and his deputies
usurped the theater,
storing their files on stage
and using one wall for target practice.
Few shots hit the golden bull's-eye.

Mike and I tour the opera house in 1983.
An architect shows us townsfolk
how restoration will transform
the pockmarked plaster
into a palace of art.

The construction crew knocks down one wall
to attach a community center.
Late at night, a rattling freight train
nearly makes the whole structure collapse.
Half the town watches as workers reinforce the foundation.

In 1986 the opera house opens again.
The former jail is now a carpeted ladies' room.
Pocked theater walls are re-plastered and re-painted
in the original design.
Our children, nervous, put on a new play.

SNOW POEM

I am searching for a poem in the snow....
As I walk, languid flakes cover familiar images,
bringing me metaphors
in crystalline form.

I pass trees like giant white flowers.
Among their branches, the light
plays hide and seek.

Fog bites off the heads of distant buildings
like a hungry dragon.

Snow arches over windows and doors,
sketching bushy eyebrows and moustaches.

Cars huddle like moles,
blinded by the storm.
Bicycles become cubist statues.

Like a witch, I will hoard
all the silent images
for my next winter brew.

MOONSTRUCK

I

Moonrise: a white sickle
mows the darkness.

II

The half-moon stretches
raw and red,
a wound at the horizon.

III

Ducks fly north,
their wings brushing
the face of the full moon.

IV

Clouds strum the quarter-moon
like a harp.

APRIL CONCERT

The red-breasted thrush
warbles a love-song
to his pregnant lady
from the top of a sycamore.
She yodels back in antiphony
from her perch
on a nearby elm.

They sing so gaily
that a German shepherd
leans out the window to listen.

FOLK CONCERT, KALAMAZOO, MARCH, 1996

Hippies with grey hair
and rounding bellies,
we listen to Anne Hills
belt out folksongs
and we stare at one another.
Something is lost.

At Camp Birch Trail, we girls
sang folksongs every day
after meals, around the campfire,
and on canoe trips.
"Michael, row the boat ashore,
hallelujah!"

I remember my first folk concert.
One spring Judy Collins came to campus,
her long black hair swinging
as she strummed or bowed,
her face as pale as trillium.
"I've looked at love
from both sides now."

Then Pete Seeger traveled to Oberlin College.
He praised the school
for hosting him during the blacklist
under McCarthy's reign of terror.
Seeger sang from his heart
and coaxed us all to sing:
"If I had a hammer,
I'd hammer in the morning."

I transferred to Wisconsin,
supported the T. A. strike,
marched in Washington against the war in Vietnam,
and sang folk music with friends.
"The answer, my friend, is blowin' in the wind.
The answer is blowin' in the wind."

Uprooted to Chicago,
I went to the Folk Festival with Mark
and Grant Park concerts with Michael.
Holly Near and Ronnie Gilbert sang duets
and the crowd joined in:
"We are young and old together
and we are singing for our lives!"

Married, transplanted to DeKalb County,
Mike and I heard the Berrymans,
savored their sublimely playful lyrics.
Our record and tape collection
kept outgrowing our cabinet.
I played Sally Rogers' paean for her grandma:
"Pretty Agnes, won't you come with me?
We'll be married in style."

Then we returned to Old Town
to hear Jean Redpath
bring Scotland's history to life
in patter and song.
I buy her tapes
and the complete *Poems and Songs* of Burns.
"But soon may Peace bring happy days
and Willie hame to Logan braes!"

Tonight, Irish midwesterners play reels and jigs—
I wish we could dance in the aisles—
and a bluegrass band strums my heartstrings.
Anne Hills's clear soprano voice floats over Kalamazoo
while the sun stands still.

Any minute, I expect a musician
to announce the next anti-war rally
or a peace vigil
or a march on Washington,
to sing in protest.

But Nixon and Johnson are dead,
Vietnam a new trading partner.
We grown flower children
mourn for our youth,
yet we keep singing.

OTHER ANAPHORA LITERARY PRESS TITLES

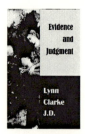

Evidence and Judgment
By Lynn Clarke

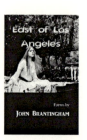

East of Los Angeles
By John Brantingham

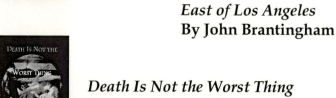

Death Is Not the Worst Thing
By T. Anders Carson

The Seventh Messenger
By Carol Costa

Rain, Rain, Go Away...
By Mary Ann Hutchison

Truths of the Heart
By G. L. Rockey

Interviews with BFF Winners
By Anna Faktorovich, Ph.D.

Compartments
By Carol Smallwood

CPSIA information can be obtained at www.ICGtesting.com
Printed in the USA
BVOW061708280512

291163BV00001B/4/P

9 781937 536268